MW01592042

# Moments and Memories from the Farmer's Daughter

## a.k.a Growing Up on the Farm

### by Betty Lou Lew

DORRANCE
PUBLISHING CO
EST. 1920
PITTSBURGH, PENNSYLVANIA 15238

Dorrance Publishing Co
585 Alpha Drive
Pittsburgh, PA 15238
Visit our website at *www.dorrancebookstore.com*

ISBN: 978-1-6461-0795-7
eISBN: 978-1-6461-0696-7

# Contents

# Introduction/Preface/Dedication

This publication was conceived/born at the suggestion of my daughter-in-law, Susan Lew (Mrs. Robert Lew). While visiting their home in Indianapolis in 2016, she suggested I tell my grandchildren (their children) Lauren and Jordan, who were present, about growing up on a farm.

I then realized my other granddaughters, Jessica and Alexandra (Branch and Marcia's children) were not familiar with farm life either, so this book was written and dedicated to all of them.

Once I started, I chose to enlarge by encompassing more of my life, thus a somewhat condensed autobiography with a few pictures.

Note to my grandchildren: I prepared a scrapbook in 1987 of my life with many pictures, which can be viewed any time.

This edition is primarily about growing up on a farm and the difference from city life.

# Birth

It all began when I was born at home in Perrysburg, Ohio. I am an only child due to my mother having a very difficult pregnancy and spending the last three months in bed to "save the baby." Unfortunately during that time she lost her mother (my grandmother) and she was never told until after I was born. What a difficult time that must have been for her. She had her first child and no mother to consult with for any of the situations that occur with new babies. My parents lived very close to my father's parents, which I am sure was a big help, but not like your own mother. Thus, I never knew my maternal grandmother. As I look back, my mother's parents lived about twenty miles from the Emch's (my father's family) and there were not as many visits there.

1

# My Family

My father had two brothers. One passed in early childhood, but his younger brother, Rolland, and my father were both farmers. The Emch clan was large and farmed many acres in the Perrysburg, Ohio area. My father always felt second best, as his younger brother seemed favored. Some of this was timing. When my father married and was ready to start farming on his own, there was no rentable land available near the Emch clan, but when Rolland was ready, there was land available in the Perrysburg area. Thus came the move to Michigan for my father.

My father did not graduate from high school and worked on the family farm instead.

Uncle Rolland and wife, Irene, had two children, Rolland Emch Jr., also a farmer, and Shirley, who married a non-farmer and had two children. I never knew her well.

My mother had two brothers, Harry and Glen Steensen. Her father was a small farmer and his sons were both in business endeavors—accounting and banking. Uncle Glen also had an interest in music. His wife Huldah may have had an influence there, as she was an excellent piano player and they formed a dance band with their son and daughter. Charles drummed and Ginny sang. My mother idolized her brothers, especially Harry. My mother graduated from Business College and also worked in banking.

Both families were of primary German heritage and attended Lutheran churches.

Uncle Harry had one daughter, Eileen, who was an English professor at Southern Methodist University in Dallas, Texas, and later in life met my best grammar school friend, Marilyn Lipp, after she moved to Texas from Blissfield. They became best friends, as they were both lesbians— what a small world!

Uncle Glen had two children, Charles and Virginia. Both married and had children. Charles worked in a factory, but I am not sure of many details in these families.

My paternal grandfather was one of fifteen. My father's mother was not such a large family. I only remember one brother, and he did not reside in the area. I do not remember ever meeting him.

My mother's parents lived in Latchie, Ohio a small rural community. We never spent a lot of time with this side of the family, but we always shared Christmas time. I remember going to the Emch Christmas dinner. Daddy took

Mother and me to her family, and then Daddy drove home forty miles to feed all the livestock and returned for another big dinner and the long drive home.

When my parents were first married, they lived in a small two-story house next to the Emch homestead, and my father worked in a factory in Toledo, Ohio. Then my father decided to move out on his own in farming.

# Move

When I was two-and-a-half years old, we moved to my rich uncle's country farm and house in Riga, Michigan, approximately forty miles north from Perrysburg, Ohio. The move was necessary due to unavailability of rental farm ground near the Perrysburg area where my father's whole family owned or rented farms. I know it must have been difficult for my father to move away from the Emch clan.

# Explanation of "Country House"

This was before the era of air-conditioning, and since my rich uncle resided in Toledo, Ohio proper, it was customary for affluent "city" folks to either go to the country or lake area for cooler air, away from the heat of concrete pavements and tall buildings, which blocked air flow in the summer months.

The country farmhouse consisted of thirteen rooms, an entrance with a marble fireplace parlor, one bedroom downstairs, a huge kitchen with pantry, and dining and living rooms. Upstairs was all four bedrooms and one inside bathroom. Most neighbors had no inside plumbing or electricity at that time. There was a full basement with generator, cistern (holding reservoir for catching the rain water from the eaves.) There was a full kitchen, root cellar (area on edge of the basement with dirt floor for storing vegetables from the garden and meat we had butchered). The winter temperatures kept things very cold, but usually did not freeze.

In the summer, the "city" women cooked in the basement where it was cooler, and the men sat outside under the shade trees and smoked cigars. There always seemed to be a breeze in the country. We had a windmill, large telephone that hung on the wall and rang by cranking. Everyone listened in on all conversations (party line). This property had a two hole outhouses—most only had one—and was fully equipped with both Sears Roebuck and Montgomery Ward catalogs which served as "wiping" paper; doubling as early sex education. Boys read all the women lingerie pictures, and girls read all the men's pages!

Attached on the next page is a map indicating the approximate distance from Perrysburg, Ohio, home of the Emch clan, to Riga, Michigan where my rich uncle's summerhouse was located. This should provide a better vision of the distance involved.

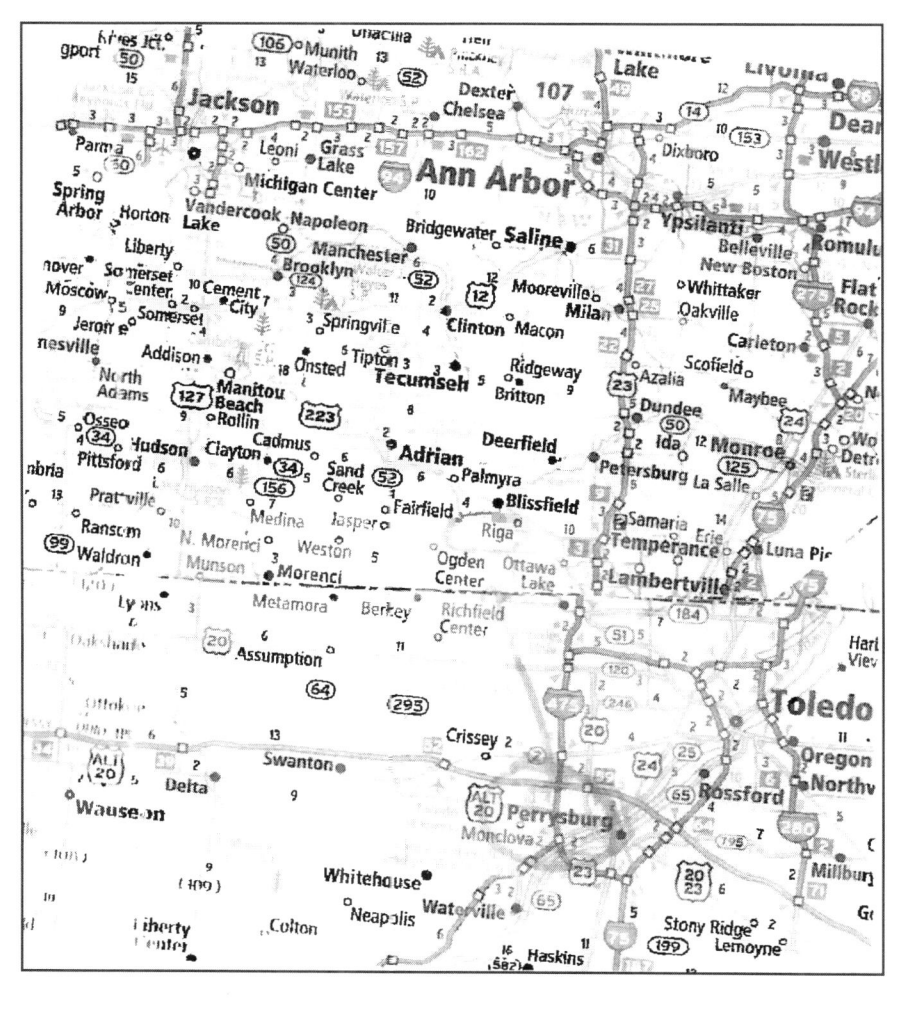

# Memories

One summer a swarm of bees flew into one pillar of the porch right by our back door entrance and decided that was to be their new home. This caused a dangerous situation, as we used that entrance exclusively, so my father and a neighbor closed all the holes in the pillar but one and gassed them with car exhaust fumes. No such thing as exterminators then—at least not in the country.

As an only child, I grew up as part boy and part girl—a helping hand to both my parents. That gave me a lot of boy and girl skills, which I did not appreciate so much then, but certainly have proved worthwhile in my adult life. Example: See me driving a tractor with tomato hampers to Riga to be sold to the Campbell Soup Company. Daddy always said I was his best tomato planter. That was meant to make me feel better about missing my senior trip, as that was scheduled during planting season. Mother always had a saltshaker in the tomato field when we were picking, and she ate tomatoes like apples.

Me driving tomatoes to Campbell's Soup loading dock in Riga, Mi.

This farm was located near a Penn Central railroad track. It was ironic I should spend a career on the NS railroad later. My dad always wanted to be an engineer on the train. I worked as an engineer when the engineers were on strike for seventy-eight days.

Back then bums (non-working men) would ride the boxcars of freight trains from town to town. My mother always fed the bums and our property was marked as a food stop. The engineer would slow down or even stop so they could pick up food and get back on the train quickly.

My dog, Buster, loved to chase trains, not cars, and my mother would whack him with a broom when he came back from chasing. She said, "Buster Dirty Bum," but she never really hurt him.

My only playmate and friend lived on a farm located on the other side of the tracks. I was not allowed to walk over there, but Daddy would drive me quite often. My friend, Cleantha Rehklau had two older brothers, Ken and Herb. The younger one would take us to school with a horse and sleigh when the snow was too deep for bikes. She also had a player piano, and we spent many hours playing and singing while our parents talked. We have kept in touch all through the years. We both married, raised families, and grew apart some, but after coming to Florida, Bob and I encountered her and her husband at the Holiday Inn cocktail hour in Bradenton. Then we started attending Lenawee County Days annually and were reunited with many other classmates. Surprisingly, many of them also wintered in this area of Florida. When we were young, we did many winter things playing, ice-skating, and sledding (there was no farm work to be done in the winter), and as mentioned earlier, riding the sleigh to school when snow was too, too deep. Only tractors with lug wheels and horses could get through. I looked forward to those sleigh rides then.

Living in the country as we did, there was not much opportunity for playmates, except in school. My dad played a lot of ball with me. I have memories of being on a softball group in Riga, which played evenings after farm work done. I would attend evening baseball games with my dad in Blissfield and sometimes saw friends from school there. Daddy and I played a lot of pencil/paper games. (i.e. tic-tac-toe (old cat), dot game, and of course, rummy). We played rummy for hours.

Examples of T,T,T, and OC:

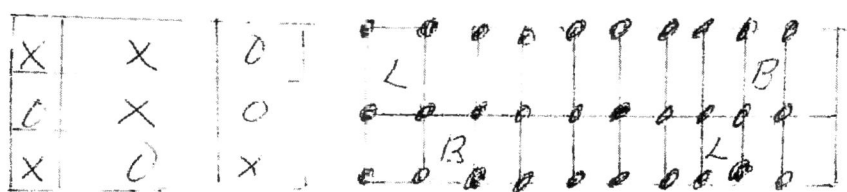

15

Cleanth at the player piano

Ice Skating

Cle & me ready for ride to school in the sleigh

Me driving Tomatoes to Campbell Soup loading dock in Riga, MI.

# More Memories

We went to Riga on Friday nights for free movies and popcorn. The outdoor "theater"—a screen and bleachers /chairs—was held in the parking lot of my parents' friends' (Jack and Laura Edmunds) grocery store. I looked forward to this and always enjoyed whoever was there as well.

I only remember one family "vacation" when I was out of school in the late summer, before fall harvest and the start of school. It was the only time to leave the farm after all the planting was completed. My dad decided we could take a vacation to northern Michigan. I was excited—we may be staying in motel. We left early on a given day and guess what? We were home that evening! When we reached the straights of macking, it was necessary to board a ship to cross to the Upper Peninsula. Daddy said, "No way," and thus turned around and headed home. I was a little disappointed to say the least.

I remember when we had German war prisoners as labor on our farm. There was a camp in Blissfield where they resided and came to the farm in a big open truck. Mother had made coffee in huge metal pots and used metal cups to serve and accompany their brown bag lunches. They picked tomatoes on our farm. Daddy had me dressed like a boy and stuffed my hair under my cap, as he was worried about the prisoners bothering me. One prisoner said, "How old is your daughter?" I guess they weren't fooled.

Eating "out" was almost unheard of. Daddy would go to Nellie's Tavern in Riga—five miles away—on Friday night sometimes, and bring home a really nice fish dinner for us. That was a special treat. Mother and I were not allowed to go to the tavern.

When I was in high school, Goetz's Snack Bar opened and was an after school hangout. Mother could always tell if I had been there after school because of the grease smell on my clothes. That was the time that French fries were introduced, at least in Blissfield, Michigan.

After all work was done on Saturday, we bathed and got all dressed up and went to town in Blissfield. We had to get there fairly early to get a front row parking place on Main Street. People walked the main drag and some people sat in their cars and watched the parade of people. People-watching was a big thing! When I got old enough to drive, some of my girlfriends and I would go to town and not park, but drive round and round the block—looking for boys, of course.

# Younger Memories

I remember taking a "bath" in a copper boiler in the kitchen by the wood cook stove that provided heat and hot water in a "well" container on the side of stove.

My mother never allowed animals in the house, but one spring we had a large litter of pigs and I was allowed to keep the runt, who had trouble getting up to his mother's table with all his brothers and sisters. I kept him in a shoebox behind the cook stove where it was warm and fed it milk with my Betsy Wetsy doll bottle. As soon as it was able to stand and move around, out it went to join the family.

I remember making homemade ice cream in a manual turning freezer. This was a frequent occurrence. Families got together and it was a "together" event. My mother always made brownies. It was tradition for the younger children to turn the freezer in the early stages (when it was easy), and the adults completed the turning when it was more difficult.

Every Sunday was spent attending Sunday school while my parents attended the service, and then we traveled to my Grandparent Emch's home in Perrysburg, Ohio, approximately forty miles away. I always changed from my good Sunday school clothes to play clothes. I usually only had one "Sunday" dress and didn't want it to get dirty or torn. I had a lot of fun playing with Shirley and Jr., my Uncle Rolland's children. I loved to play an RCA Victoria my grandmother had, and it was a manual. We would play big records and sing along. Also, I loved to gather the walnuts in her driveway and get green stains on our hands, another reason for changing clothes. We also played card games like marbles and Parcheesi.

Grandmother always cooked a fowl, beef and pork every Sunday with homemade noodles, still drying on the dining room table from being made Saturday,. She had pie, bread pudding, cookies, and never knew exactly how many were coming but always prepared plenty.

Grandma and Grandpa argued a lot, mostly over her egg money and how she spent it. Both of the sons, Leo and Rolland, argued with Grandmother about her Sabbath, as she was a Seven Day Adventist.

Even though there was verbal abuse, Grandpa never touched or hurt her physically. I never really saw them hug or kiss each other in the presence of others. He bought her very nice things, built her a nice new home with a full basement, dumbwaiter, stenciled walls, new Mixmaster, Packard auto.

Explanation of dumbwaiter: hand pulled elevator shelf for bringing things up and down from the basement such as canned goods, etc. It was always my job to use the new Mixmaster and mash the potatoes. I guess I have been mashing potatoes for a long, long time! At our house, we used a hand masher or ricer for potatoes

My parents were very demanding, loving, disciplined, hard-working individuals who instilled in me a great work ethic, morals, loyalty, thoughtfulness, gratitude, religion, and many other good attributes.

I really don't know if one is "born" or "trained" to be a morning or night person. I am obviously a morning person and always have been. I attribute this partially to the necessity of early rising to do chores before going to school. There was no choice, as I remember it. Saturday was always a busy day with lots of other chores to be done in the summer: cleaning, washing the car, mowing the grass, etc.

Many a Sunday, Daddy and I would play rummy card games at the kitchen table as mother fixed dinner. Daddy always ate the chicken gizzard, and I got the heart. We shared the liver. We did this on Sundays we did not go to Grandmother Emch's.

We would listen to Michigan games on the radio—Detroit Lion football and Detroit Tiger baseball—while playing rummy. Sometimes if it was a nice day in the fall and no heavy farm work to be done, Daddy would ask me to go to Ann Arbor, Michigan with him, approximately forty miles north, to a University of Michigan football game. I loved doing that. Mother did not care for sports. I remember one Saturday when we went he bought me a beautiful yellow chrysanthemum with a blue "M" on it. What a treat—and we would always stop in Saline, Michigan at a home-style restaurant for a bite before we got home.

My parents were friendly with several other couples and they would get together and play horse pepper (a card game) and when they met at our house it was my job to make grilled cheese sandwiches for everyone when it was snack time. They drank highballs (whiskey and 7-Up).

My parents also went bowling with this same group on Saturday nights, and all us kids would stay at Harold Goetz's house who had a teenager that would babysit us and play games until our parents got home. What fun.

On Saturdays, mother and I dressed chickens. Mother would chop their heads off and hang them by feet on the clothesline to let all the blood drain out. It was my job to get the bucket of hot water (with Mother's help) and de-feather and pick pin feathers from the chickens. Then my mother would dress them, or remove the innards from them. There was never a cleaner chicken inside than my mother's. She washed them out with ivory soap after removing the innards.

We also made Parker House cinnamon rolls and bread, which Daddy sold to the city folk in Blissfield.

We raised our own chickens, which my father could not wait for the pullets to be large enough for Sunday dinner. Every Sunday we had fried chicken the way I still prepare it, using my mother's method, with mashed potatoes, home made biscuits, gravy, and vegetables from the garden.

Our stove had a deep well in place of one burner, and that was a great place to keep mashed potatoes warm after mashing. I still think it would be a nice idea.

We also sold eggs to a German bakery in Toledo, Ohio, and Daddy would take dozens of eggs there weekly, and he would return with warm chocolate éclairs—what a treat.

We also grew and sold potatoes to Kuhman potato chip factory in Toledo, and Daddy would take potatoes and return with a large metal can full of warm potato chips. Mother and I made little pigs of ourselves. I still love potato chips!

Both my parents were hard-working people. Since farming was a volatile endeavor and dependent on weather, seasons, etc., my father worked other jobs (i.e., Whirlpool (Ypsilanti, Michigan), Anhydrous Ammonia Plant (Blissfield), Hay Mill (Blissfield) and drove a truck for Kraft cheese. All this was in the winters.)

My mother went back to work at local bank in Riga, Michigan, when I was in high school.

# More Memories

We had a lot of animals on our farm—pigs, cattle, chickens, milk cows, horses, sheep, and my father had a favorite pair of horses named Pat and Mike, strawberry roans. He thought they were so special. He would hoist me up on their backs for a ride once in a while.

Every spring we went to the hatchery and purchased baby chicks. My job was to keep the water bottles filled with some kind of yellow stuff, which was to keep the chickens healthy.

We were very fortunate to have electricity in our house. However, each room had one light bulb in the ceiling. I think this was where I developed my dislike for ceiling fixtures. I always wanted a softer lamp, etc.

My mother always ate the crust of the pie before eating the filling. She said, "Duty before pleasure."

My father instilled in me a dislike for the word "can't". I remember telling him I couldn't do a chore he had instructed me to fix while he ran an errand. He said, "Can't died in the poor house. I will be back in a few minutes, see what you have figured out."

To this day I may say, "Not sure I know how to do that, but I will try," but I never, never say, "I can't do it."

My father was a tough taskmaster, but good in his own way.

My mother was a hard worker and adored my father. I remember baling hay when it was very, very hot, and mother would bring a large thermos of water to the field. She always put some lemon in, as she said workers would not drink as much so fast and it was better for them in the hot sun. Neighbors helped each other bale.

Mother and I made lots of strawberry jam from our own strawberry patch. We also had an abundant supply of wild asparagus, which I disliked as a child and love it now.

We had a pickle crock in which we processed pickles every fall and canned them.

Mother and I would pick apples from a tree in our back yard. The apples were rather small. Consequently, there was lots of peeling to make one pie. In the fall, we would make approximately fifteen pies for the freezer. Freezers were a fairly new innovation at that time. The only other methods of preserving food were canning, which everyone did, or drying, which was not as common. I loved my mother's canned beef, which we made when we butchered. We made wonderful beef and noodles in the winter months.

Mother was quite an accomplished seamstress. She always made me a new dress for the Christmas program at church. My favorite was a large, blue corduroy, and it had two laces in front on either side. She also made some Easter dresses for me when I was small.

Pets: We had many different wild cats that were necessary to keep the rat population down in the granary, a storage area for corn. My dogs were Old Black Joe (just a dog), a white terrier named Penny, a nice collie, and of course Buster, as mentioned earlier about chasing trains.

Dolls: I do not remember very many. I had the Betsy Wetsy one previously mentioned and a very special one that was a China-German doll that was my grandmothers, which I still have and has been refurbished..

There were rough times, but we always had food. Nothing fancy, but we grew most of it and had our own cattle, pigs, chickens, etc.

Learning to cook: I learned a lot about cooking from thrashing. All the men would get together and cut, shock, and thrash the grain while the women cooked a huge lunch. Thus the expression, "eat like thrashers," as men worked very hard physically, and they ate very hardily, always a complete meal with full dessert. Cleantha and I learned a lot while peeling potatoes, setting the table, doing dishes, etc. Cleantha's mother could slice cabbage on a board with a large knife, and it was thinner than any other cabbage I have known.

Cleantha's parents were such good neighbors. I was rather sickly as a child—hard to believe now—and Mrs. Rehklau (a German name which meant "hoof of a deer") always brought flowers from her garden and baked goods to me.

As a young child I remember playing by myself a lot, helping with chores, and I liked being around animals. I learned to milk manually. There were no electric machines in my time.

Our farm was located in Lenawee County, Michigan. We grew grains, oats, wheat, barley, corn, soybeans, tomatoes, and two seasons of peas for the Soup Company.

Our well was a long distance from the house and barn, clear across road with a giant windmill. In the severe winters, we encountered the pipes would freeze. My dad had a welder come and melt ice with blowtorch.

Another thing I feel worth mentioning: I learned to drive at an early age and had a license at fourteen with some restrictions. My father taught me to drive, as there was no such thing as driver's education classes. He did a fantastic job with parallel parking and the proper backing from drives.

My formal education started at standard school. This was a two-room school, but we only used one room, and we only used the other room for Christmas plays.

Our teacher had to teach all eight grades. Each grade had their allotted time up front with the teacher, but we were all in the same room. Actually, I rather liked that, as I loved learning and could listen to some of the other grade's instructions. We had birthday celebrations and some holidays with paper napkins on our desks with popcorn, corn candy, and sometimes apples. Of course, we had recesses, which was a learning time. There was a family of all boys. About six lived across from the school, and they were pretty tough. Finally a little girl, Eloise, came along and production stopped. Dale and Herman were in my age group, and one recess Dale said to Herman,"Look at those birds fucking up on the roof." I went home and asked my mother what that meant. Wow, a big lecture!

There was another family with more than one in the class, the Osborn family—one boy and two girls. They were not very clean, and mother explained to me that was not their fault, and when I didn't want to give them a valentine, she informed me I could not give one to my friend Dee Goetz (a cute boy) if I didn't give everyone else one too!

I won the spelling contest three years in a row, but I don't remember going to a higher contest after that, or maybe I didn't do well?

Cleantha and I usually rode bikes to school except when there was too much snow and her brother Kenny took us in a horse driven sleigh—a real treat. He was a very nice older brother.

When my parents purchased their own farm, we moved to Horton Road, and I started school at Riga Elementary.

That was where I became good friends with Marilyn Lipp (another farmers daughter) and Donna Jasmund who lived in Riga, not far from school. Donna, Marilyn, and I were very close friends.

To this day, Donna—who married Norman Figy from Riga—lives in Wesley Chapel. Marilyn is deceased.

Interestingly, this took me away from Cleantha until meeting in high school. Cleantha and I have stayed in touch through the years. She was wintering in Florida close to me for years, but since losing her husband, Ward Joughlin, she now resides in Adrian, Michigan full time.

# High School

After eighth grade at Riga Elementary, we (Marilyn, Donna, and I) met back up with Cleantha and became friends with Gretta, Carol, and several others.

I attended every social function in high school—dances, all sports events, and I learned to square dance.

I wanted so badly to be a cheerleader, but since I was from the "country" and all the cheerleaders were "city" girls, I was too bashful to even try out. Hard to believe that as you know me today, right?

I met my husband in high school. He was the athletic director and coach at that time. Since I was a good student, I worked during my two study periods—one for the Principal, Mr. Pebbles, and one for the athletic director, Mr. Lew. Mr. Lew and I never dated or had any suggestion of doing so while I was in high school. Mr. Lew's basketball and track teams were very successful and provided Blissfield with championships they had never known before during high school. I remember several girls' slumber parties. At a particular one held on New Year's Eve at Harriet Rohrback's house, there was a terrible ice storm during the night, and it was very difficult for our parents to come pick us up the next day. We girls thought it was quite cool.

After I graduated from high school as salutatorian on a Friday, I started work on Monday morning at Blissfield MFG. Co. They manufactured refrigeration units for drink dispensing machines such as Dr. Pepper. I started as a receptionist and later worked for the purchasing department. There I met Kenny Jackson who was a friend of Mr. Lew and lined up my first date with Mr. Lew at a basketball game, of course. Long story short, we were married two years later.

My father did not believe in college education for girls. I credit my husband for not only giving me self-confidence, but also encouraging me to further my education. I attended my first class at Adrian College. I was apprehensive about that because I was older than the average student then, but it was fine after that first class.

At that point, I seemed to enjoy life and all the activities created by my Bob's coaching, etc., but the best was yet to come—the birth of our two sons and then a move to Fort Wayne with a new coaching position for Robert. I loved living in the city (more people to see). It was a little difficult for me to move away from Blissfield, from my friends and my parents.

I became very involved in the boy's school, Frances Slocum Elementary PTA, chairing the annual fair, and eventually becoming president of the PTA.

We lived in a two-bedroom, two-story home on Lawndale Avenue across from Klug Park. The park was ideal for the boys. They had day camp in the summer, a basketball court, and play equipment.

I started to work part-time at Koerber's Jewelry Store. I worked Wednesday evenings and Saturdays.

So Bob could stay with boys, I rode the bus to downtown where Koerber's was located, close to the bus stop.

In a few years, we moved to our larger home—three bedrooms, two baths, and a full basement on Glencairn Drive. Our sons attended Glenwood Elementary, Lane Jr. High, and Snider High School. We lived very close to all three schools, and the boys walked to and from school.

During these years, both boys became very interested, in soapbox derby racing, probably because of their father being in the derby as a child. Bob and the boys spent many hours working on the derbies. Both boys were very successful in the derby to their dad's delight, and their prize monies assisted greatly in their college education expenses.

Eventually I went to work at Collin's Oldsmobile dealership for a short time and then to Norfolk Southern

Railroad. I actually worked a short time at ATT in the personnel department before joining the railroad.

I had a great tenure at the Norfolk Southern railroad. I was the first woman to become "chief clerk to the superintendent," similar to an office manager position in other industries. I appreciated the fact that the railroad treated me well, and I received the same pay as men.

In the next years, we watched our industrious sons graduate from college, pursue their careers, get married, and raise families.

In due time, Bob and I retired and spent our winters in Florida. We were drawn to Palmetto, as my parents were residing there. We still remained in Fort Wayne for the summers and kept our home on Glencairn for many more years. We had purchased a home in Bradenton, and eventually sold the property in Fort Wayne.

# Summary

As a backward glance, I would like to say my "growing up on the farm" was very good for me. I learned great discipline from caring for many animals and meeting deadlines at planting and harvesting time. I also leanred good monetary planning what with all the expenditures being in the spring (seed, fertilizer, etc.) and no income until fall or harvest time. We always hoped for good weather to produce a bountiful crop to cover expenses and have funds left.

I learned to substitute ingredients when cooking, as we did not go to town very often—or borrow a cup of sugar or such from a neighbor.

One special trip, twice annually, was to Toledo, Ohio. Daddy would drop off Mommy and me and go visit his family, and we could shop all day. He would join us later in the afternoon and help purchase a nice outfit for my mother and me. We always visited Morrow's Nut House, for warm nuts and Tietke's where I was allowed to have some chunk chocolate from their barrel. I took chunk to cash register to be weighed—no gloves—and put it in a paper bag. Yummy!

My mother shopped from Sears/Roebuck and Montgomery catalogs most of the time. They always had plenty of cotton underwear, but I sure did yearn for the fancy lace ones.

Now, but probably not in my youth, I feel privileged to have been raised as a "boy and girl." learning many chores and skills of both lives provided me with versatility and the independency I now possess.

In youth I lamented the fact I did not have very many playmates, but my childhood friend Cleantha and I are still close today. She lives in Adrian, Michigan and is widowed also. She provided some of the pictures incorporated in this publication.

# Further

I feel life has been good to me, especially since I enjoy good health and am able to be very active. I find I am stronger and more capable than many of my counterparts or anybody my age.

**But the Very Best**

Aside from all the growing-up memories and school days, married life was great for me and provided the birth of two of the world's greatest sons, both with doctorate degrees, who together with their wives have provided four outstanding grandchildren and six great grandchildren.

I am so proud of all of them and love them more than I can say or show!

# Glossary of Sayings/Expressions

"You can lead a horse to water but cannot make him drink." You can suggest for someone to do something but sometimes cannot make them do it.

"Better late than never." A favorite of my mother's when things did not get done or written on time, do it anyway.

"Birds of a feather flock together." Meaning, you should select friends who have the same thinking as you like the birds do.

"Red in the morning, sailors take warning. Red at night, sailors delight." This was taught to me by my maternal grandmother.

"Busier than ten cats covering shit on a tin roof." This was my dad's expression meaning he was super, super busy, as it was impossible to cover shit on a roof without dirt.

"If you don't do it right the first time, you will have to do again." This was a lecture from my mother when I did my Saturday dusting in a hurry to get outside. After she inspected, I had to go back in and do it again—the right way. I think of that many times now when I am doing anything.

I remember asking my mother permission to do something that I knew she would not let me do and I said, "All the other kids get to do it." Mother said, "If sally jumped off the bridge into the river, would you?" and I could not swim.

"People in glass houses should not throw stones."

"Like calling the kettle black."

# Some Scientific Advances I Have Witnessed in My Lifetime

Telephone: from the phone on wall with a crank ringer and party line where everyone listened.

Dial phone: no operator

Cell phone: wireless and mobile

Transportation: horses, Model T Ford, gasoline engines, hybrid engines, all battery operations, airplanes, jet powered

Heating/cooling: pot-bellied wood stove, coal furnace, stoker furnace, hot water, hot air, electric heat, ice box, window boxes, electric refrigerators

Cooking devices: wood burning cook stove with hot water reservoir, electric and gas ranges, microwaves, electric skillets, pressure cookers, crock pots

Entertainment: radio, RCA phonograph record player, television—how we love TV. What an amazing advancement.

# Some Other Things
# I Remember as a Child

No television: TV came in during the 50s

My parents were quite good at puzzles, riddles, rhymes, songs, slogan, and paper games
(Examples in the appendix.).

There seemed to be a lot of "neighboring" done in those days. I always remember Cleantha's mother bringing me flowers or baked goods when I was sick.

# Appendix

**Puzzles/Rhymes/Paper Games**
**Riddles**
**Advertising Slogans**
**Lexophiles**
**Burma Shave Signs**
**Positive Thinking Quotes**

Many times while my Daddy and I walked the long trek from the house to the barn, he would have me hippity-hop and sing this jingle:

"Hippity hop (skipping) to the barbershop to get a piece of candy,
One for me, one for you, and one for baby Andy."

That was another one of those rhyming things. We didn't know a baby Andy.

It seems like the nursery rhymes of my time were more about rhyming and sometimes didn't make any sense such as:

"One, two, buckle my shoe,
Three, four, open the door,
Five, six, pick up sticks
Seven, eight, lay them straight
Nine, ten, a big fat hen, (and so on)"

"Hey diddle diddle, the cat and the fiddle
The cow jumped over the moon
The little dog laughed to see such sport
And the dish ran away with the spoon

Hey diddle diddle, the cat and the fiddle."

# Rhymes

"Rain, rain, go away,
Come again some other day.
Little Johnny wants to play"

"The itsy bitsy spider crawled up the water spout.
Down came the rain, and washed the spider out.

Out came the sun, and dried up all the rain,
And the itsy bitsy spider went up the spout again."

"Humpty Dumpty sat on a wall,
Humpty Dumpty had a great fall,
All the king's horses and all the king's men
Could not put humpty together again"
(He was an egg, of course )

"Jack and Jill went up the hill
To fetch a pail of water.
Jack fell down and broke his crown,
And Jill came tumbling after."

"Twinkle, twinkle, little star,
How I wonder what you are.
Up above the world so high,
Like a diamond in the sky."

# Riddles

Out in the field there was a mill. Around the mill was a walk,
and under the walk was a key—where am? (Milwaukee)

What is black and white and red (read) all over? (Newspaper)

I am black when clean and white when dirty, what am i? (Blackboard)

What can run, but never walks, has a mouth but never talks, has a bed but never sleeps? (River)

You answer me although I never ask any questions. What am I? (Telephone)

# Advertising Slogans

"Good to the last drop, and that drop is good too." (Maxwell House Coffee)

"99/44, 100% pure. It floats" (Ivory Bar Soap)

"You are in good hands with _____" (Allstate Insurance)

"A little dab'll do ya." (Brylcreem)

"M'm! M m! Good!" (Campbell's Soup)

"It keeps going…going…and going." (Energizer Batteries)

"Snap, crackle, and pop." (Rice Krispies Cereal)

"The breakfast of champions." (Wheaties cereal)

"Takes a licking and keeps on ticking." (Timex Watch)

# Lexophiles

I added these—do not remember doing them as a child. Definition: a play on words.

"You can tune a piano, but can't tuna fish."

"To write with a broken pencil is pointless."

"I didn't like my beard at first, then it grew on me."

"I stayed up all night to see where the sun went, then it dawned on me."

"England has no kidney bank, but it does have a Liverpool."

"Did you hear about the cross-eyed teacher who lost her job because she couldn't control her pupils?"

"No matter how much you push the envelope it still will be stationery."

# Burma Shave Signs

I always read these along the highway on the way to Grandmother Emch's house. They were prevalent from 1930 to 1960.

"He saw the train and tried to duck it, he kicked the gas and then the bucket."

"Passing school zone, take it slow, let our little shavers grow."

"A man, a miss, a car, a curve—he kissed the miss and missed the curve."

"The midnight ride of Paul for beer led to a warmer hemisphere."

"Don't stick our elbow out so far, it may go home in another car." (Note: There was no air conditioning in cars then. Windows were open a lot.)

# Positive Thinking and Attitude Quotes

I like to think of myself as a very positive thinker, so here are a few of my favorite quotations for your thought tank.

Most of these were taken from *Positive Charges* by Alexander Lockhart

"I also value the word 'attitude' a great deal."

"Ability is what you're capable of doing. Motivation determines what you do. Attitude determines how well you do it." (Lou Holtz, former ND football coach)

"Attitude is the mind's paintbrush. It can color any situation."

"Any fact facing us is not as important as our attitude toward it, for that determines our success or failure." (Norman Vincent Peale)

"There is no danger of developing eyestrain from looking on the bright side of things."

"A positive mind finds a way it can be done. A negative mind looks for all the ways it can't be done."

"Always affirm to yourself that there is a solution to any problem and that you can find it."

Grand Champion Showgirl with Herford Steer

# BLISSFIELD HONOR STUDENTS

Miss Margaret DeLoach

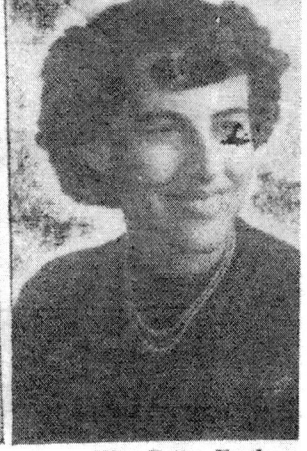

Miss Betty Emch

Special To The Telegram

BLISSFIELD, June 2 — Miss Margaret DeLoach is the va
torian of the 1951 senior class of Blissfield high school. Miss
Emch has been named salutatorian. The class will graduate T
day. Miss DeLoach, daughter of Mr. and Mrs. Duane DeLoach of
field, has been active in dramatics and the school band as well
her studies. Miss Emch, the daughter of Mr. and Mrs. Leo Em
Route 1, Riga, also was active in school plays and the band.

Salutorian Credit from Newspaper
Adrian Daily Telegram, Adrian, Michigan, Saturday, June 2, 1951

WINNER OF MRS. R. S. V. P. CONTEST 1995

Betty Lou Lew

BLISSFIELD HIGH SCHOOL MARCHING BAND

I played first chair clarinet in
The Blissfield High School concert and marching band.

## SOME OF MY ACCOMPLISHMENTS I FELT MY GR ANDCHILDREN SHOULD KNOW

WINNER OF SPELLING CONTEST IN ONE ROOM SCHOOL THREE CONSECUTIVE YEARS.

GR AND CHAMPION SHOW GIRL IN 4-H WIT H ANGUS AND HERFORD CATTLE ( AGE 10-14)

FIRST CHAIR CLARINET IN MARCHING AND CONCERT BAND OF BLISSFIELD HIGH SCHOOL.

SALUTORIAN OF GR ADUATING CLASS AT BLISSFIELD HIGH SCHOOL.

WON BEAUTY CONTEST IN 1995 AS MRS. RSVP (RET IRED SENIOR VOLUNTEER PEOPLE)

DANCED AND CHAIRED THE STRUTTERS WITH THE SUNCOAST MUMMERS AND STRUTTERS GROUP OF BRADENTON FLORIDA.

ASSISTED ROBERT LEW IN RAISING TWO OF THE MOST FANTASTIC SONS, WHICH PRODUCED FOUR WONDERFUL GRANDCHILDREN —MY PROUDEST ACCOMPLISHMENT OF ALL. – BEING THEIR MOTHER AND GRANDMOTHER.

# Family

My Parents
Leo & Margaret (Steensen) Emch

# Grandparents

William & Ada Emch

Andrew & Rosa Steensen

# Aunts and Uncles

Uncle Rolland, Aunt Irene (the daughter Shirley)

Uncle Harry, Aunt Lily, My mother

# Cousins

Charles & Ginny Steensen
Children of Glen & Huldah Steensen

Dance Band: Composed of Uncle Glen, Aunt Huldah, Charles and Ginny

# Cousins

Rolland Emch Jr.
Junie and Shirley Emch
Children of Rolland & Irene Emch

Eileen Steensen
Child of Harry & Lily Steensen

# 'Mystery Farm' of Mar. 10 Identified
# As That of Mr. and Mrs. Leo Emch

The Blissfield Advance
March 17, 1955

The farm of Mr. and Mrs. Leo Emch, of Riga, located on East Horton Road a half-mile off Barkey highway, was identified by a number of Advance readers from the picture in our "Mystery Farm" series published March 10.

Mr. Emch owns the 60-acre farm, on which he does general farming, and also works for the R. J. Ireland Alfalfa Mill. He purchased the farm in April, 1946, from Jacob Zeizert. It was previously owned by Fred Maierle, and his parents, Christian and Regina Maierle.

The first owner, Mr. Emch recalls, was a colored man who bought it originally from the government, and every four years he walked to Washington to be present at the Presidential inauguration. After he sold the farm, he walked to Washington again to see the new President.

Mr. Emch and his wife, the former Margaret Steenson, were married April 11, 1931. Their only daughter, Betty Lou, is now Mrs. Robert Lew. They are members of St. John's Lutheran church in Riga, of the Blissfield Masonic lodge, and the Lenawee County Farm Bureau.

Leo's favorite hobby is bowling. He's on Tine Shedler's team in the Blissfield Bowling League.

He prefers raising alfalfa among other crops on his farm, but also raises some wheat and oats. He has no livestock at present.

MY FATHER'S FIRST FARM

HORTON RD . BLISSFIELD MICHIGAN

# Marriage

Mr. & Mrs. Robert Lew
(Betty Lou Emch – Robert Lew)

# Mrs. Betty Lew Serves As Chief Clerk

## *Fort Wayne Woman Fills Job That Traditionally Has Belonged To Men*

Mrs. Betty Lew's husband is a high school math teacher and she has a son in high school and another in college. She cleans house, prepares meals and performs all the duties typical of a housewife.

But employees of the Norfolk and Western in Fort Wayne, Ind., consider Mrs. Lew somewhat of an expert on the ins and outs of the rail business.

Even though she has ridden a train only twice in her life, railroad lingo and train operations are as familiar to her as instructions in a cookbook.

She knows the rail business because she is the chief clerk to the superintendent of the Fort Wayne Division of the NW. For a typical housewife this is anything but typical. Within the transportation department of the NW, there are 22 chief clerk offices but Mrs. Lew is the only woman to head such an office. So she is anything but typical.

"I don't think of my role as women's lib," she said recently in a telephone conversation. "I think of it as an opportunity for an individual to do the best job that individual can."

As a child she lived in a rural Michigan area near a railroad track and that's about as close as she came to trains until she boarded the old Wabash Cannonball for a short trip from Fort Wayne to Adrian, Mich., almost 12 years ago.

Now she spends a lot of time answering telephone calls from NW personnel checking on traffic and the position of shippers' cars. The telephone calls also are from people inquiring about leasing railroad property or buildings or from realtors wanting to know how many trains cross various streets or crossings.

"You definitely have to have a feel for public relations," is the way Mrs. Lew summed up her job. Something the chief clerk has learned since she has been with the NW is "respect for those trains at crossings! I don't take them for granted any more."

Betty Lew

While being able to type certainly is no handicap, basic requirements for the job of chief clerk are a knowledge of train operations and knowledge of different positions within the department.

"And," she added, "you have to know the lingo. A gondola from a boxcar, a flatcar from a tri-level."

She joined the NW in 1967 as a budget clerk. She learned that work and also did payroll work "and filled most all vacancies during vacations." Traditionally on railroads most clerical positions have been filled by men, so two years ago when the chief clerk in Fort Wayne retired it was very much against tradition for Mrs. Lew to be named to the position.

"But the NW has been opening up doors for women for sometime now. That's definitely a good idea because there are many areas on a railroad where women, if qualified, can perform just as well as men."

When Mrs. Lew joined the railroad there were six other clerical positions in the office. Men held four of these positions, now there are only two positions held by men.

"I don't sense any resentment," she said in a soft and pleasant voice from the other end of the telephone. "I have experienced no problems on my job because I am a woman in a traditional man's job. Everyone is really wonderful and they couldn't be more helpful. This job can definitely be handled by a woman.

"People used to say that railroading gets in your blood. And I'd say 'maybe for you, not for me.' But now I feel a little different about that. I really enjoy this work."

One of the things she enjoys about her position is "the variety. Every day something happens that didn't happen the day before."

As for the duties that go with her job, she answers nearly all the department's correspondence and handles accounting, payroll and employee services. She answers phone calls for the superintendent that can be about almost anything, since the superintendent must see that freight cars get on the right trains.

"I think of myself as a career woman because since my two sons are older I am not confined to household duties. I will probably work for a long time because I enjoy this. It would be dull without my work."

The work frequently involves late hours or weekend work but Mrs. Lew has not found this disrupts her household. "My husband (Robert) pitches in when he has to but I don't think the job has ever really caused any problems or disrupted any of my family activities."

Two trips from Fort Wayne to Adrian may not compare with the rail miles that many veteran railroaders accumulate before they retire but already Mrs. Lew has learned a lot about rail operations.

She has learned enough to make her interested in every aspect of railroading. Now she said she would like to hitch a ride on a caboose and get a different view of railroading. **NW**

19

# Railroad Memories

Five other retirees from NS Railway when I retired.

Office Staff

Me with James Willard, engineer for the steam excursion

...THRU THE YEARS

# These 2 Youths Use Soap Box For Derby Quest, Not Protests

**By RICHARD O. BACON**

Who says our youth are "going to hell on roller skates"?

Just between us, I can't buy that theory.

Our youngsters today are traveling at a pretty fast clip, I'll admit —s o m e to-ward maturity, accomplishme nt and self - satisfaction; others to-ward trouble, d e g r a d a-tion and f a i l-ure.

Richard O. Bacon

But by a wide major ty, they are going in the right direction FAST!

Take, as an example, a couple of young "hot rodders" that I know — two brothers who live at 3037 Glencairne Drive.

In a time when newspapers, magazines, radio and television are fi led with stories of youth in revolt and trouble, Branch and Bob Lew are like a breath of fresh air.

Branch, 11, and Bob, 14, sons of Mr. and Mrs. Robert Lew, haven't been stealing hubcaps or pitching bricks through windows — but their story, and others like it, deserve being told and retold.

In a time when it's "mod" to get up on a soap box and shout about how sick t h e world is, Branch and Bob have taken the soap box and used it for a different purpose.

Last September, they started working on their cars to be entered in last month's All-American Soap Box Derby.

The Lew brothers had a rich heritage in Soap Box Derby racing — their father had been runne -up in the 1937 and 1938 races, back in the days when Fort Wayne had its own Derby competition.

But since Fort Wayne has not had Derby competition for several years, it's difficult for youngsters here to find a city to enter the race.

In April, 1967, the Lews started correspondence to find out how and where the boys could enter a race car. National All-American Soap Box Derby headquarters in Detroit sent a list of locations of races in the area. Indianapolis a n d Marion Derby fields were restricted to entrants from their districts.

Finally, and fortunately, a letter came from Muncie Derby officials, welcoming the Lews to enter. As the boys' attractive mother described the happy reaction, "We stopped writing and he started building!"

Last year, Bob started building his car in April (Branch was too young to enter) and it took him 3½ months to finish it for the July race. He won his first heat race, but lost his second. He gained experience, though, as well as a trophy for the best "out-of-county car."

The Lews went to Akron, O., for the International Soap Box Derby finals last year anyhow. As the boys' dad says, "We were scouting, getting some ideas and wanted to improve last year's standing."

Branch and Bob worked nine months in the basement, using trial and error. They finished building their respective race cars on July 11, the night before the official weigh-in at Muncie.

Ninety-three cars were entered in that race. The winner had to win six heats (two cars per heat race) to win the championship. Bob ran in the 11-12 year old category; Branch in the 13-15 division.

In a one-in-million chance, Bob and Branch each w o n

their class!! — Precipitating a dramatic head-to-head confrontation of two brothers competing for the big prize. One they had both worked hard on for nine months.

Imagine the elation the boys and their parents felt. But how would you feel if you faced your brother as the last barrier to the race title? How would you react if you were the father or mother of the two finalists?

Branch admits "I was kinda' nervous" before the last race. "We shook hands and wished each other luck."

He won the championship and the right to run in the Internationals at Akron on Aug. 24 for the world champianshp. He received a $500 Savings Bond, the championship trophy and the trophy for best "out-of-county car."

Bob, winner of the runnerup trophy and lots of respect too, couldn't have been happier that, if he had to lose, his younger brother won.

The boys are like that— champions, both, in every way! Champion Branch is a straight-A student at Glenwood Elementary, plays L i t t l e League baseball, and m o w s six lawns in the neighborhood each week. Bob, a 9th grader at Lane Junior High, gets "more As' than B's." Both play on their school and PAL basketball teams.

Branch wants "pretty much" to win the Aug. 24 championship, becoming Muncie's fourth Internationals Champ (F o r t Wayne's first; Indiana's 9th). We'll all be pulling for him!

But, the next time you hear someone saying "youth is going to hell on roller skates," remind him about Branch and Bob Lew, two clean-cut kids who are going the other way— toward achievement — on WAGON WHEELS!!

# Various Living Facilities During My Married Life

Rented Carpenters
Cottage
Blissfield, Michigan

113 Quick St. Blissfield
First Home Purchase

2210 Lawndale Dr., Ft. Wayne, IN

3037 Glencairn Dr. Ft. Wayne, IN

3801 21st Avenue West, Bradenton, FL

# Most Current Photos of Branch Lew Family

LATEST ADDITION TO BRANCH LEW

FAMILY – BORN 2/19/2020

ROBERT  LEW FAM